THE WATER IS TROUBLED

JUMP IN

BREAKING OUT OF STAGNATION

Zenene Humphrey-Davis

Dedication

To God, my loving Father in Heaven, who literally snatched me out of my mess and placed me on the path to holiness, faith filled living, and purpose. To my husband, children, mother, and mother-in-law who remained encouraging during this time of birthing.

To the mindset architect herself, Coach Candace B. Woods, thank you for seeing in me years ago, what I didn't even see in myself. Thank you for never giving up on me.

Thank you all for pushing and believing in me.

Foreword

Show Your Faithfulness

Candace B. Woods

The Water Is Troubled, Jump In: Breaking Out of Stagnation is an incredible book that is a true testimony of perseverance by its author, Zenene Humphrey-Davis. I had the pleasure of meeting Zenene roughly three years ago while embarking upon my journey of becoming a full-time entrepreneur. We instantly connected and she shared her heart's desire to start her ministry. I didn't really know her story, but something told me that she had an amazing testimony. And to be honest, this book is only a small part of what God has in store for her.

Over time, I was given the pleasure of becoming Zenene's mindset coach. I've watched her allow God to stretch her and develop her into who she is called to be. Every step that she has taken over the years, although they may have seemed small to her and others, they were one step closer to her living out her purpose and her calling. Many obstacles were thrown her way, trials came, and fears would often creep in and cause her to lead with caution. But there is one thing she did not do. She DID NOT STOP.

As you read this book, I encourage you to do as Zenene has done and take a self-assessment of where you are in your process of discovering your true self and your purpose. Be honest with yourself about where you are and where you desire to be. Allow the words from this book to touch your heart and inspire you to do the work to begin to build momentum and choose to no longer remain stagnant. Leave with the determination to be a good steward of the life, time, resources, and purpose you've been given by God by showing your faithfulness. Keep going. Keep showing up. Whatever you do, don't give up until you see the manifestation of the promises of God.

Table of Contents

INTRODUCTION

How long? Not long. A quote my old pastor used to say about the length of time we have on this earth. You know, he was right. We all believe God for long life. Some people live to be 110 and that is amazing! However, even that is not a long time. The Bible tells us that our lives are a vapor, that appears for a little time (James 4:14 paraphrased). The sad part about this is that we spend a significant amount of this time procrastinating and making excuses for why we are not moving forward into our destinies, our goals, and into all that God has for us. We may hear a good prophecy and know that it is from God. Yet, we cannot seem to take that first step. God may give us visions and dreams. But we can't seem to step into them. Don't get me wrong, there will be times when God will have us in a waiting season. However, this is totally different from our own self-sabotaging behaviors. God's waiting season is never to be confused with our own fleshly procrastination. God never intended for us to be stagnant, stuck. Stagnation leads to a life of

\regret and missed opportunities. It detours us from purpose and from destiny. It can keep us from the deliverance and healing that our Father in Heaven wants us to experience. It keeps us from getting all that is stored up for us. It can even cause those connected to us to become stuck as well.

Statistics show that 80% of people never set goals for themselves (Douglas Vermeeren, Reliable Plan) and even more devastating, of those who do set goals 70% fail to achieve them.

You do not have to stay on this road that has seemed to close. You do not have to turn around and go back because the road seems to have been road blocked. You can come out and move forward. You can be who God is calling you to be! Start your engine and buckle your seat belt. We are going for a ride.

I will not tell you that this ride will be a smooth one. But I will tell you that you can do all things through Christ who strengthens you!

I will not tell you that you will not face opposition. But I will tell you that there are more for you than are against you.

I will not tell you that the enemy will not try to remind you of who you once were. But I will tell you that you are who God says you are!

Ready... Set... Let's go!

Notes:

What do you hope to gain in reading this book?

____

____

____

____

____

____

____

Notes:

What do you hope to gain in reading this book?

CHAPTER ONE

Are You Tired Yet?

CHAPTER ONE

ARE YOU TIRED YET?

Stagnation, according to Merriam-Webster.com, is defined as a stagnant state of condition: a state or condition marked by **lack of flow, movement, or development.** I remember as a teenager going on a long trip with my family from Montgomery, Alabama all the way to Cincinnati, Ohio for a funeral. My great uncles had chartered a bus to make sure that everyone who wanted to go on this trip could go without having to worry about transportation. Well, all was well on this journey until suddenly, we stopped moving. As we leaned over our seats to see what was happening, we saw that there were two tractor trailer trucks, one in both lanes of traffic, that decided to slow down to about 10 miles per hour. This left every vehicle behind the trucks, including our bus, with no choice but to slow down to an even slower pace it seemed. At first, we all just kind of chuckled and nonchalantly mentioned the slow pace and wondered what was going on. We wondered why these trucks were moving so slow. After moving at the same pace and often having to stop completely to avoid an accident, we all became more and more concerned. Quite quickly our concern turned into frustration and frustration into anger. However, the longer we stayed stuck, the more we became used to moving slow or not moving at all. Sometimes we get so used to not accomplishing things in our lives, we see it as our norm. Wonder what would have happened if we had sought out a different route, a detour, another way to get moving or maybe even prayed? Maybe we would have gotten to our destination a lot faster than we did and with a lot less frustration.

Life is often like this. We start out with goals and great intentions but then we hit a roadblock and instead of seeking direction, we just stay there. We fall into the trap of stagnation and if we are not careful, we will never move from that place. Thinking back on that long day of travel, by the time we made it to our destination, we were all so very tired.

John 5: 5-6(NIV), One who was there had been an invalid for thirty-eight years. When Jesus saw him lying there and learned that he had been in this condition for a long time, he asked him, "Do you want to get well?" I believe what Jesus was saying to him is "are you tired yet?" My question to you is are you tired yet? You may have been in this place 2 years, 38 years, or 55 years but nevertheless, nothing changes unless you want it to. Nothing changes until you make up in your mind that you will not waste another day, another hour, another minute feeling sorry for yourself or making excuses. Nothing changes until you are no longer comfortable where you are.

It is time to say yes! Yes, I am tired! Yes, I am ready! Yes, to God! Yes, to your purpose! Yes, to your destiny! Yes, to what God wants you to do! Write the book! Apply for the job! Start the business! Join the small group! Lead the small group! Write the song! Preach the word! Register for school! Whatever your yes needs to be, it is time to respond to God with a resounding YES!

I challenged you to reach way down in your sanctified soul and give Him a YES!!!

Procrastination is exhausting. Setting goals and never making steps towards those goals is crippling. Are you tired yet?

Open your heart, open your mind, open your mouth, and tell God yes.

What does saying yes entail or indicate? It indicates that you let go of your will for God's will for your life. It indicates that you surrender your way for God's way. It indicates that you subject your thoughts, ideas, and actions to Him. This is not easy. It goes against our very nature. We tend to want to be in control of all these things. We want control. But if this is how we have always operated and have only found ourselves stuck then it is time for us to do things differently. We have all heard or read somewhere that doing the same thing repeatedly and expecting different results is insanity. So why do we continue doing things the same way we have always done when we see clearly that it is not working?

We were not put here on this earth to just go to work, come home, pay bills and repeat. We all have a purpose. So, I ask you again, are you tired yet?

You have not gone through all you have gone through to not help someone else get through. You have purpose. Are you tired yet?

You are not having visions and dreams to not act on them. Are you tired yet?

You didn't write out that business plan just to look at it year after year. Are you tired yet?

You didn't buy all those books on the shelf about that topic just to collect dust on the shelf. Are you tired yet?

You didn't make resolution after resolution just to do what everyone else is doing at the start of each year. Are you tired yet?

Enough is enough, it's time to move.

Now that you know these things, you will be blessed if you do them. (John 13:17)

Notes:

What do you need to say yes to?

____

____

____

____

____

____

CHAPTER TWO

Obedience is Better Than Sacrifice

CHAPTER TWO

OBEDIENCE IS BETTER
THAN SACRIFICE

When we say yes to God, we open the pathway for Him to do amazing things in our lives. However, saying yes is only the beginning. We must listen and obey what God is telling us to do. One act of obedience can change your entire life.

In 2019, I felt the Lord was calling me to move away from my hometown to another city. I was offered a job on the same day that I interviewed for it and accepted the job before even thinking it all the way through (that was probably a good thing). I was a little fearful of moving away from my family, knowing that I only had one person in Auburn, my dad, and he always stays busy. My kids were not ecstatic about the move. They knew they would have to make new friends and attend new schools. I didn't have much money and was unable to find a place to live that was ready to move into. However, I felt in my spirit that this was a God move. I pushed aside my fears and made steps to transition. Everything in the natural and some of those people closest to me were totally against the move. You see to the natural eye; I was moving out of a house into a hotel. I was taking a job that only paid a couple dollars more than what I was already making. I was uprooting my children. Against all odds, I knew this was a move of God, I just did not know how big of a move. Long story short, one act of obedience allowed God to give me two promotions within seven months. I went from not having a bed to sleep in to having a place to live in a great area, with plenty of space, with brand new furniture in every room, and a child who is doing what no one thought she would do, graduating from high school in exactly four days from the time I am writing this. God not only gave me an Executive Director position at an agency after only seven months, but He also turned my pain into purpose and increased my territory in a way that allowed me to be a blessing to others and to those who had been a blessing in my life when I did not have anything.

If I had not obeyed the Lord and made the move that I made at that appointed time, I would still be stuck in a city that I could not seem to prosper in. I would be stuck with an income that barely allowed ends to meet. My daughter would have been stuck in a school that she barely attended and when she did not attend, no one noticed. Stagnation can be downright detrimental to your wellbeing and to the well-being of your children, family, etc. Obedience is far better. Easy? Of course not. It is not always easy to be obedient to the things God is calling you to. Obedience is often uncomfortable, but the blessing on the other side of your obedience is priceless. The blessing on the other side of fear is miraculous. One act of obedience can change the lives of your whole family. One act of obedience can change your city, your state. A whole nation can be changed by your yes and your willingness to obey God. Do not stay stuck. Move! Even if you must go alone, go. Everyone cannot go where God is taking you. 2 Corinthians 6:17(NIV) says "Therefore, come out from them and be separate, says the Lord. Touch no unclean thing, and I will receive you." Sometimes God will call us to a separation. It may be because there is too much "noise" around you where you currently are that you cannot hear Hirn. Distractions can cause us to become stagnated. It may be because you have become more dependent upon those around you and less dependent upon the Lord. The voices of those around you sometimes drown out the voice of God. Whatever the reason may be, the key to moving forward is obedience to the voice of God.

"There are far, far, better things ahead than any we leave behind." -C.S. Lewis

Have you ever wondered exactly what is meant when the scripture (1 Samuel 15:22) says obedience is better than sacrifice? Think about it. When you make a sacrifice, you are making a decision, a choice to offer something. It could be your time, your money, your belongings, etc. But when you are obedient, you do what you are asked to do despite whether it is your choice. Often, what God is calling us to do does not start out as being something we "choose" to do. As a matter of fact, it is often the exact opposite or so far away from what we thought we would be doing. Often, this is because we don't see ourselves the way God sees us.

When obeying God, we need to obey Hirn with a good attitude about it. Obedience to God leads to growth in every area of our lives. Disobeying God, however, leads us into stagnation and a simple business as usual way of life.

You may be wondering how you can know if you are obeying God. One thing I will tell you, read and get to know His word. Find yourself in the scriptures. This is the most important way that you will know. He will never tell you to do anything that contradicts His word. Obedience is so important to receiving the promises of God and being able to enjoy heaven here on earth!

It all goes back to your relationship with the Lord. Build and cultivate your relationship and you will know when He is speaking. Seek Him and seek Him diligently! It is a daily walk and a daily privilege.

But seek first his kingdom and his righteousness, and all these things will be given to you as well. (Matthew 6:33)

Notes:

In what areas of your life do you feel you may have been disobedient? If you are anything like me, this list is tough but just like you, I am striving to change that every day.

____

____

____

____

____

____

____

LORD, WE WILL OBEY YOU BECAUSE WE LOVE YOU!!

CHAPTER THREE

No Excuses

CHAPTER THREE

NO EXCUSES

John 5:7, "The sick man answered him, 'Sir, I have no man to put me into the pool when the water is stirred up; but while I am coming, another steps down before me.'"

When I read this passage of scripture, I see excuses. We all have them, and we all have used them.

I have a past. I used to do this. I used to do that. I still struggle sometimes with that. I don't have time. I don't have that degree. I can't speak well in public. I don't know the Bible like her. He is a pro, and I am not. I don't have anyone to watch the kids. I've never led an agency. I don't speak well like he does. I wasn't raised to do that. My father wasn't around. My mother wasn't around. My husband left. My wife left. I don't have what I need. I don't... I don't. We literally talk ourselves out of the purposes that God has for our lives. I am not saying these things aren't true and I am not saying that these things don't hurt us or cause us to see voids in our lives. However, the sooner we learn where our strengths and abilities come from, the better off we will all be. Our strength comes from God. It isn't about what we can or cannot do. It isn't about who was in our lives or who wasn't. It isn't about who hurt us or who left us. It is not even about what we feel like we want to do. It is not in our own strength. It is not about us. It never has been about us, and it never will be. We have to learn to move us out of the way and allow God to work in our lives. We must stop making excuses. Use that pain for purpose and multiply!

I mentioned earlier on how I made a transition from one city to another that allowed my life and the lives of those around me to be blessed. Well, do not think for one second that I did not make excuses that almost stopped me from getting the position that changed our lives. I made every excuse I could think of before putting my name in the hat for the Executive Director position. I had never written a grant. I saw how frustrated others became in this position. I did not know much about leading, hiring, public speaking, domestic violence awareness, outreach efforts, etc. Thankfully, I had my husband and other kingdom minded people in my ear who spoke against every excuse I made. They reminded me who made me and who was able to supernaturally teach me everything I needed to know to do well in the position if it was His will for me to have it. I have successfully led the agency for almost two years since.

What excuses are you making for not obeying God? For not moving forward in ministry. For not taking steps towards your destiny. Put an end to those excuses today. We often use excuses as a pacifier, as a way to stay in our comfort zones.

"All progress takes place outside the comfort zone". -Michael John Bobak

Move yourself out of the way. Stop making excuses. Stop talking yourself out of your destiny.

"Put all excuses aside and remember this: you are capable". -Zig Ziglar

Remember you are capable. Tell yourself, write it on a sticky note and put it on your mirror, tape it to your wall, shout it from the roof tops, whatever it takes, "I can do all things through Christ who strengthens me." (Philippians 4:13 NKJV).

I decree and declare that you will not another day make excuses for why you aren't doing what God is calling you to do. You are more than a conqueror!

When I think about the excuses that I have made in my life, I am reminded of how long they kept me stagnated. Maybe you have dealt with and may be still dealing with some of these same excuses. Let's put them to rest right now, today! I challenge you to an act of faith. Write those excuses down. Yes, write them down. Now destroy them. It's an amazing act of faith.

CHAPTER FOUR

But how? I Can't Swim

CHAPTER FOUR

BUT HOW? I CAN'T SWIM

Say it with me, "It is okay to get help."

The world, or maybe it's just us, will have us afraid or hesitant to get help. God will not only call you to do things, but He will also place people in your path to help you along the way. Don't be afraid to reach out and grab that help. Your help could be your spouse, your parents, a friend, a pastor, a leader, or even a coach. I was tremendously blessed that God allowed me to connect with my coach, Candace B. Woods. She coached me over the years and later became the bridge that helped me birth this book that you are reading. Even after I accepted the position as Executive Director at my job, God placed people in my path who were able to assist me. He didn't leave me hanging and neither will he leave you. "Be strong and courageous. Do not be afraid or terrified because of them, for the Lord your God goes with you; he will never leave you nor forsake you." (Deuteronomy 31:6)

In my career there were and still are times I must humble myself and if there are things, I am not sure of, or just simply hard days where I don't know which way to go, I ask for help. It doesn't make me any less successful.

Don't be afraid to get help from those whom God has strategically placed in your path. He doesn't expect you to jump right in and swim perfectly. He knows that there will be days you need your life jacket. He knows there will be days that you will need to reach for the edge of the pool. He just wants you to jump on in. He wants you to act on your faith. Notice I said to act on your faith. We can have faith and never act on it. He wants you to move.

There are some things He supernaturally showed me, but there were some things I had to reach out about. It's okay. It doesn't reduce your value, it doesn't mean you aren't called. It doesn't mean you missed it. It doesn't mean you're not where you're supposed to be. Stop letting the enemy wrap you up in shame. That is another trick to keep you stuck.

Even some of the most prominent people in the Bible had help. God knew Moses personally. He allowed him to come face to face with him. The word even tells us that when Moses died, God himself buried him. Yet, God gave Moses some elders to help him.

But the Advocate, the Holy Spirit, whom the Father will send in my name, will teach you all things and will remind you of everything I have said to you. (John 14:26 NIV)

The Holy Spirit is a teacher of all things, and He will also lead you to those who can assist you.

There are tons of free as well as paid trainings, books, and information out there for you. I highly recommend a coach of your choice for accountability but use what works for you.

Notes:

Who are some people you can reach out to that will hold you accountable for breaking out of this stagnation that has held you hostage?

____

____

____

____

____

____

CHAPTER FIVE

3 Tips for Breaking Out

CHAPTER FIVE

3 TIPS FOR BREAKING OUT

Tip One: Calm the Noise

Some of us just have way too much going on. We are saying yes to everything and everyone except what God wants us to say yes to. I challenge you to examine your life and everything that you have going on in it. Eliminate some things that are just space fillers. Are you working fifty plus hours on your job like I used to do just because you can, and not necessarily because you must? Commit yourself to only working over when it is absolutely necessary. You will be surprised at the difference going home on time will make. I learned that the hard way but once I learned how to do it, I had more time to work on mygoals, invest more time in prayer, bible study, and connecting with others.

Disconnect yourself from anyone and anything that is drowning out the voice of God. No one has to tell you; you already know who those people are and you already know what those things are. If you don't calm the noise, it is going to be difficult for you to break free from stagnation.

Do you know that the enemy will send distractions to keep you stagnated and to keep you from your purpose? What is a distraction? It is anything that prevents you from giving full attention to something else. It is also extreme agitation of the mind or emotions. Identify the distractions and commit today that you will not be distracted.

Calm the noise.

Tip Two: Seek the Lord

I cannot stress enough how important this is for breaking out of stagnation. It is a sure way you will be able to break the stronghold of stagnation off your life. Ask the Lord in prayer. Don't be afraid to pray specific prayers. Prayer is essential to breaking free from stagnation.

Prayer doesn't change God, it changes me. ~C.S. Lewis

Set aside time to pray, worship, praise, study, etc. I must reiterate, the Lord will never give you instructions that contradict His word. So, it is super important to read your word. Ask God to open your spiritual ears to hear Him. If this is not something that has been a normal part of your day, I will give you some advice, even if you start with 5, 5 and 5. Five minutes of word, five minutes of prayer, and five minutes of worship every morning. Just start somewhere and grow from there. This was one lesson I was taught in church that helped me grow in my prayer life. Find a quiet place, slow down, take time to lay before the Lord and listen. He's always speaking. Ask the Lord for wisdom in moving forward.

If any of you lacks wisdom, you should ask God, who gives generously to all without finding fault, and it will be given to you. (James 1:5)

The beginning is the most important part of the work. -Plato

Do not despise the small beginnings, for the Lord rejoices to see the work begin, to see the plumb line in Zerubbabel's hand. (Zech. 4:10)

Tip Three: Commit

It may sound simple to some and a bit scary to others but commit. Commit today. Commit to God and commit to His will for your life. Commit to yourself. Make yourself a promise that you won't waste any more time. Commit to yourself that you will not over-commit yourself to things that may be good things but are not necessarily God's things. Commit that you will watch out for things sent from the enemy as distractions to keep you so busy that you end up stuck all over again. Commit to no longer sitting at the edge of the pool making excuses. Get accountability partners who will help keep you on your toes.

Truly take these tips and apply them to your life. Use them daily. Even when you don't feel like it. Press in! It is time to break out of stagnation. It is time to move. The water is troubled. JUMP IN!

Notes:

Write out your commitment and your vision for yourself.

____

____

____

____

____

____

____

WHAT DOES GOD SAY ABOUT STAGNATION?

The Lord our God said to us at Horeb, **"You have stayed long enough at this mountain.** Break camp and advance into the hill country of the Amorites; go to all the neighboring peoples in the Arabah, in the mountains, in the western foothills, in the Negev and along the coast, to the land of the Canaanites and to Lebanon, as far as the great river, Euphrates. See, I have given you this land and the Lord swore he would give to your fathers-to Abraham, Isaac, and Jacob-and to their descendants after them. (Deuteronomy 1:6-8)

For this reason, I remind you to fan into flame the gift of God, which is **in** you through the laying on of my hands. (2 Timothy 1:6)

Remain in me, as I also remain in you. **No branch can bear fruit by itself; it must remain in the vine.** Neither can you bear fruit unless you remain in me. (John 15:4)

All Scripture is God-breathed and is useful for teaching, rebuking, correcting, and **training** in righteousness, (2 Timothy 3:16)

Let **perseverance finish its work** so that you may be mature and complete, not lacking anything. (James 1:4)

Every good and perfect gift is from above, corning down from the Father of heavenly lights, who does not change like shifting shadows. (Jarnes 1:17)

But seek **first** his kingdom and his righteousness, and **all** these things will be given to you as well. (Matthew 6:33)

The thief comes only to steal and kill and destroy; I have come that they may **have life and have it to the full.** (John 10:10)

My sheep **listen** to my voice; I know them, and they **follow** me. (John 10:27)

For we do not have a high priest who is unable to **empathize with our weaknesses,** but we have one who has been tempted in every way, just as we are-yet he did not sin. (Hebrews 4:15)

Brothers and sisters, I do not consider myself yet to have taken hold of it. But one thing I do: **Forgetting what is behind and** straining toward what is ahead, I press on toward the goal to win the prize for which God has called me heavenward in Christ Jesus. (Philippians 3:13-14)

Strive to see yourself the way God sees you and push past the lies that keep you stuck!!!

JUMP IN!!!!

BREAKING OUT JOURNAL

I mentioned previously that we should find ourselves in the scriptures. In this section you will find the same scriptures from the section "what does God say about stagnation". This time, instead of just reading the scriptures, find yourself in them and write down what He is speaking to you.

Enjoy and embrace the move!!!

The Lord our God said to us at Horeb, "**You have stayed long enough at this mountain.** Break camp and advance into the hill country of the Amorites; go to all the neighboring peoples in the Arabah, in the mountains, in the western foothills, in the Negev and along the coast, to the land of the Canaanites and to Lebanon, as far as the great river, Euphrates. See, I have given you this land and the Lord swore he would give to your fathers-to Abraham, Isaac, and Jacob—and to their descendants after them. (Deuteronomy 1:6-)

____

____

____

____

____

____

____

____

____

____

For this reason, I remind you to **fan into flame the gift of God, which is in you through the laying on of my hands.** (2 Timothy 1:6)

Remain in me, as I also remain in you. **No branch can bear fruit by itself; it must remain in the vine.** Neither can you bear fruit unless you remain in me. (John 15:4)

All Scripture is God-breathed and is useful for teaching, rebuking, correcting, and **training** in righteousness, (2 Timothy 3:16)

Let **perseverance finish its work** so that you may be mature and complete, not lacking anything. (James 1:4)

Every good and perfect gift is from above, coming down from the Father of heavenly lights, who does not change like shifting shadows. (James 1:17)

But seek **first** his kingdom and his righteousness, and **all** these things will be given to you as well. (Matthew 6:33)

The thief comes only to steal and kill and destroy; I have come that they may **have life and have it to the full.** (John 10:10)

My sheep **listen** to my voice; I know them, and they **follow** me.
(John 10:27)

For we do not have a high priest who is unable to **empathize with our weaknesses,** but we have one who has been tempted in every way, just as we are-yet he did not sin. (Hebrews 4:15)

Brothers and sisters, I do not consider myself yet to have taken hold of it. But one thing I do: Forgetting what is behind and straining toward what is ahead, I press on toward the goal to win the prize for which God has called me heavenward in Christ Jesus. (Philippians 3:13-14)

____

____

____

____

____

____

____

____

____

____

____

____

____

ABOUT THE AUTHOR

Zenene Humphrey-Davis is a wife, mother of three, and a DV survivor. She is now the Executive Director of a domestic violence program, and published author.

Zenene is a prayer warrior who has seen firsthand what the power of prayer, worship, and the word can do. She has watched God change her life and uses all that she has been through for His glory. She is committed to seeing others free!

She is the daughter of Walter and Bobbie Grove and a proud graduate of Alabama State University, where she graduated with honors in 2008.